Even the Fawn Has Wings
Cherie Geauvreau

Brick Books

CANADIAN CATALOGUING IN PUBLICATION DATA

Geauvreau, Cherie, 1948-
    Even the fawn has wings

Poems.
ISBN 0-919626-71-8

I. Title.

PS8563.E38E8 1994   C811'.54   C94-931202-9
PR9199.3.G43E8 1994

Acknowledgements: 'in the carnival behind the eye,' *Poetry Canada Review*; 'the shadow of the crow,' *The American Voice, The Capilano Review*; 'straw doll,' f(*lip*); 'shut your hole...,' 'the onion song,' *Prism International*; 'instruments of wood & wind,' *Snapshots, Black Moss*; 'a poem for two sisters,' 'locus,' 'twentysome,' 'cantabile,' *The Capilano Review*.

The support of the Canada Council and the Ontario Arts Council is gratefully acknowledged. The support of the Government of Ontario through the Ministry of Culture, Tourism and Recreation is also gratefully acknowledged.

Cover art by Adrien Town. Author photo by Trish Birney.

Typeset in Trump Mediaeval, printed and bound by The Porcupine's Quill. The stock is acid-free Zephyr Antique laid.

Brick Books
Box 38, Station B
London, Ontario
N6A 4V3

to the memory of
Alexis Bishop
1955 - 1985

Contents

The Carnival Behind the Eye

Moonmilk

Middle Distance

The validity of my life
is whether you read this poem
or not
and whether it speeds
your arrow.

– Dorothy Livesay

The Carnival Behind the Eye

wedding snapshots: 1944 *the jiggerbug stops*

a sailor wed to light   to love
so incisive   so quick

it is the snake scabbard & blade
inscribed on his skin   he is

war dancer   passion man
at the end of his bluing arm swings

the stanchion and lash his marriage will be
pressed against him   the bodiced rose

the wreathed palm   oblations of bone
transfixed within the folds of time

graduation snapshot: 1963   men of the house

chests out
        chins in
                shoulders back

hands cup the balls the marbles the family jewels
(dicktracy dicktracy dicktracy)

toes point   eyes squint   brows knit
light splits legs into ribbons of black

sunshine soaks hair from thin to thick
behind the suits and hard ribs

a fiddler's bow heart
        a minstrel's tender loss
                a sheer hitter's love of downbeat

the price

big brother plucks and pokes and baby's eye unleashes, pops
softly, rolls. he scoops it up, shoots it like a marble across the
floor.

mommy hears the ricochet (this echo, this vision stone). she
toes and rolls it and takes it to the sink. she scrubs it, shakes
it and dries it on the sill between the legs of a wishbone.

the eye reflects its bit of light. it prods the shadows and
depths of the empty room all day long. daddy whistles a
tune. he plunks tincan boogie on his excellent guitar.

baby squats for days, a soft finger in the socket. squats and
grows tattoos. arms briskets of blue. screendoors slam. the
furnace hums. the other eye concusses, sucks in. even so,
night never comes.

vocation

once when I opened my mother's door a crucifix of steel
pierced my right hand. fallen, flown, it had buried itself in
bone, a spear ashine in the cap of golgotha.

I wept. I was moved by the flinty crown and silver feet. the
ache and shame like sweet pulp in his disfigured face. I grew
my skin to wrap him, warm him in living flesh.

I bore him to table but no one saw as I drank cups and cups
of madness in red.

mother twisted away. father was trapped in song, I waved my
christ uselessly over the melody. I knelt beneath my
brother's fist and offered the cross to him. he mocked this
new deformity, this sin so great.

the left hand began to do everything: to cover the mouth, the
eye, the vulva. the left hand (Verso), closest to the heart,
grew and grew. the right hand (Jesus), planted in bloodstone,
averted death forever. amaranth.

windsor/detroit: waterfront july 1967

4 white girls blow down
shug down to dee troit river
oil banks   to thick water
cragged in orangewhite flame   down
to watch 12th street burn

all night and all the next day

no trees
no cotton
no brush fires
just ghetto for kindling
feeding the heat

later we learn of firemen
fire men dropped in heaps
at snoot's end
of rooftop pistols

we are pale canadian
and borderchoked
but over we go
when the bridge reopens
we chase tank tracks

buy Colt 45
and drink in the deepest corner
of tiger stadium
my airforce american uncle

languishes in the bleachers
rugged under the lights
television screens pop, sizzle, crank
out the news:
the bengals lose again

in the carnival behind the eye

it is what I see
to the left, red in black
a smudge of colour transcribed
from the night to the glass

it is what I write
translations from red to black
to light, black again;
circum/scribed dead/line

it is who I see
for some time, life is this
(unrecognizable)   un/recognized;
hands riding a prayer wheel

it is what I live
in the phantasm of the red gash
in the carnival behind the eye
dimming inward, pro/lusion, pro/lapse

it is all I am
preliminary trial, occlusion
sucking through the pursed hole,
dis/sembling in the glass

child of mine

she learns to lie still
secret air lifts her to light
to distant cracks
in her small life

where fingers claim her brow
where lips brush her nape
where greatgods soak her lungs
with weeping

she has hands but no arms
and in her face
the eye incandesces
bright split worlds

she lies still
she doesn't cry
behind the eye
even the fawn has wings

a graceful dance in quarter time

through the glass down the hall
I can see her babysoft skin
    unknown to herself but old news
to the compte & comptesse
    as she floats across tiles
threads columns   straddles balustrades
    so public so humble so sweet
she has been defiled but no one remembers
    no one can quite recall
for the dance is too immediate
    she is seven eight nine
and spreads out like veils in all the windows
    teddybear thighs grind glass
chubby fingers pierce the cave
    her eyes throw themselves and bounce
like poetal stones taptap   taptap

silent sheathes

and speak poetry?   like hope?   like eyes vaulting upward
into the heroic?   like every time I say yes the answer is
no?   or go ask the night where cocks loom like trees

I'd ask my friend but she can't talk   with her tongue in my
mouth   do I go back?   to the living symbol   the repetitious
mark   the X on the spot   the hidden larynx

paraclete of love

my body
the dangerous beast
kills to eat
chews a finger
gnaws a hand
sucks its teeth

> the wall
> the gate in my brain
> gales of blood
> thunder through
> flood the ears
> swallow the heart

> my shadow
> snagged in half-flight
> pinned by needle moons
> drugged by the sun
> sleeps in fits
> and magnifies the lord

a poem for two sisters
for M. and A.

your legs leibling
roped and snarled
to the spindle chair

your arms schwester
scarlet wings
that lathered the air

         your simeon   your dachau
your mother's incantative trance
your father's razor smile

your sister's heart
cured with lye
and stretched hard
over your round mouth

        the skin of the drum they beat on

your tears
the sound of rain
slashing down
the throat of the sparrow

scrimshaw

these pages are marked   polygraphic tentacles   quivers and
slashes   snakes and ladders   systolic evidence of a sly cloud
slung just below the heart

overhead outside   jets streak back and forth   back   and
forth

where in China is it safe to write   where in Chile or
Guatemala   Iran   Iraq   Northern Slovenia   Indian River?

I know places in Alberta where it is not safe to write   murky
words sail within bottles neatly stacked   in a cold
cellar   next to baby beef liver

everywhere: the pulling of the string   and what are in those
pockets of resistance   coins?   languages?   screams?   or just
tongues

women and men pin yellow suns to their front door

the shadow of the crow

I he slipped in and out of blue rooms and basements a
dangerous man between conjugal beds & i dreamed always in
white with the radio on & i dreamed the little flower of
jesus the redflesh of longing child of the assumption i
confessed blessme blessme father for i have and this is
my first communion why am i not Immaculate Immacula
when I carry this fist of faith in my vagina

but then i was Black Maria White Chanteuse and i danced
the Rosary March on the 1st of May forgiving the
Redeemers their sexual liturgy epistolean abuse and i
chanted gaily in the rhythms of tainted saints 'o cum o
cum let us all sing latin sing latin' genuflections of the
heart custodies of the eye

father brother christ on earth of all the deaths i could've
had but i was the Holy One Daughter of Light swallowed
in cassock black and now my long livid silence sings for the
cross in the floor the hail & hymn of the sacred
place where lie buried the soiled panties of a child blessed
beloved relic

II if i write it down if i make it legible readable speakable if i
state it as truth will it be real will my mind will my eyes
the protectors be penetrated will light leak in like acid and
burn through the wall of my brain do the pictures start
then do the words come and come borrowed stolen
usurped no more

will these legs walk with me will these hands i've never
known reshape release and heal from the touching they've
made will these breasts stop burning and floating and
freezing in sound like soft bones can i have years can i
have times can i have the thing disarmed arrested

will the thin tight lip of my rage bleed open   open   will the
words (broken skin) peel away   whispers into wind   or will
horizons steam into my mouth like dawn or love or night

III   he said   the heart beats like ice beneath the shadow of the
crow

IV   i answered in many voices: we are the face of
tribulation   we are the mouth of the cave

Symptoms present: drive over a cliff pull a trigger roll off a
ferry in foetal position   Out of Order: time sleep lists so
many lists and eat eat eat   hallu hallucinations medications
habituation   names all the names   And Body Parts: rage
swells the shoulders   fear howls down the wrists   pain
sleeps in the heel   fingers palpate torn bits of time   the
fugue   Things never quite right: yes we are Catholic good fat
nun het het hetero   mommy baby gone   such a pretty face
below that bright incisive mind   we   tried to be born
again   good news   not enough caritas   charis ma   bent
under   the spirits the tongues the healings the miracles   and
even then the surrender would not come

V   she ran backwards at the speed of night   she didn't drown in
sadness   she soared through it   Beauty and Obscenity cut
her equally   they were one   a double-headed   burl-handled
axe

VI   cut the killing rope and   up she went   through slipstreams
and striata

27

VII but the writing yes   the writing   undertow pulling me
back   pulling down and the writing   a stillness   a density
utterly without wing

the onion song

I   compelled if not by jesus
who waves at us with his friday arms
while kneedeep in the convulsions of that love

    then by truth?
or the countenance of truth?

    fused visions reduce
    the eye constricts   contracts
    and we stare at the blind spot
    until light pikes the eyelid open

II   compelled if not by jesus
and his shock in giving birth
'They're coming!' his uterus slamming shut after us

    then by fear?
or the memory of fear?

    his surplice shifts
    like scarfskin falling away
    we are babies   still keening against
    the hock and heel of what has gone before

III   compelled if not by jesus
who looks just like me
his anguish distasteful   his language stuffed into wrists

    then by courage?
or the meaning of courage?

    girls with golden brains
    whose wombs are cracked and licked clean
    sing valour between the lips of children
    adagios before the music begins

iv   compelled if not by jesus
whose opulent heart plummets
and burns and scorches the airwaves

    then by faith?
or the intimation of faith?

    despite the burning tire
    beaten black around our necks
    a poet scripts fingerboned fire
    a paladin ride like wind in her lungs

v   compelled if not by jesus
and his father's attempt to dulcify
our daughters' rocking antiphony

    then by love?
or the transcendence of love?
    i'll sing and you'll sing
    and in the slightest of times
harmonies of birth will reemerge
the chant of a child already born without pain

straw doll

looking at her now   this looking makes me sleepy   just
want to sleep too much constant wakefulness   trying to
keep ahead of   but this is the end   my mother's dying   so I
say everyone   everyone's dying   it's tiring

I read poems to her   lean to her seashell ear and flick hair
away from her nose   eyebrow   she never seems to notice
but this hair drives me mad   I want to rip it off like strands
of an old corn broom   hair in your face I want to
hiss   doesn't that bug you   but I just read and lightly
flick   she loves the drums of Plath most of all

tiger balm by the bed   I dab her temples   her yellow eyelids
flex and tic   I touch the bone of her skull   feeling the lumps
like misshapen knuckles beneath her scalp   I know her
face   flat plane at the cheekbone   lips of ash

once a bubble blew gently down the corner   not enough to
slide across her creaking jaw   she didn't wake   didn't
swallow   didn't part lips with her swollen tongue   the
bubble dried   to crust   to black

arms thin   elbows like buckles   skin smooth as cherry
wood   I rub   I rub her body   enchant the pain and
uselessness   snake charmer

I wasn't tired before   never slept   I took a fever to her
bed   pinched her toes   this little piggy   then the
next   seeing my heat infuse   I believed it

best was my hand on her chest   in the crux   with only a
film of skin between breastbone and heat   I forced into
her   through her to the sheet   cupped her spine   she was so

but she kept right on dying   now I'm tired   want to flip that
blanket back   get in   lie down on her pineboard body   cover
up   sleep

not long to go

I know her inside out   I know parts   parts that twist and
cling   I know the taste in the pit of her throat   I know
where the air is   the empty spaces   muscles of dust   cinder
bones   straw doll   I could set fire to her

I must be dreaming   must be asleep   hard to know

I caress the jar in my hands

open it

sweep two fingers   circle circle   hot and smooth

I eat   I sleep

she's running through all the rooms of the house   my
brother's pants slapping her back   she's holding them over
her coffee coloured hair   in triumph   he's hot on her heels
yelling   clawing her waving arm   mom mom give me back
my damn pants/   not till you say you're sorry/   aw mom
come on please/   kiss me? no?   kiss me!   and he does   on
his knees   kissing her feet   choking on laughter   she
tousling his hair

I am awake   in back of my eyes I see her then   young
together   like sisters   like fun   trading make-up   smokes
black velvet   everyone said   yes   you could be sisters

mom   when

I sleep

tiger balm slinks out of my grasp   thuds the floor   she's still
there   not

daddy vague   twining fingers up the back of her white silk
blouse   sunday morning kitchen   ham in the oven   in the
livingroom gram swilling sherry   snapping gin
rummy   brothers exploding noise from the basement   me
on

stairs   panting   out of sight   between adult and
child   watching my parents play their hunger

mommy

body so deep hot and soft   fingers pucker in my mouth

I waken   I stand   look down at her   lean   my ear cups her
mouth for a breath   a signal   there   I sit and scoop tiger
balm   replace the lid   roll the jar in my hands

rolling dough

rolling hands

both hands meeting round my chest   lifting me like pudding
into a bowl   poking my tummy   kneading my chubby
thigh   cold stinging me to alarm   she sings   washing
me   washing me   fingers pattering the water   making me
laugh making me squeal   I kicksplash   pummeling her
sweet hands   her wrapping me forever and I lolling content
on her lap

when was this dream   when

now

she snorts   her breath trapped away from her lungs   awake I
am watching her   she growls   tries to bounce the breath
loose   free the air to go down down   but it's lodged up there
in her mouth   lashed to her teeth   did I forget to take her
teeth out

mom

mommy   wake up and breathe

mommy   wake up

locus

having been given the scourges
   along with the rooms

and each room with eight doors
   leading out and open

revealing the levels of stairs
   and every stair striding up

to the roof and its peristyles
   we lay our blankets down

arrange our dial and stones
   like simeon   and hear

only faintly from the world below
   the suicides relentlessly turning

we've come up and away from obloquy
   the sewn lip   the blunted tongue

and their songs inciting us to joy
   or to write until the dead are dead

so as not to offend
   we've come up to you   oversoul

sweeter and higher   and deaf
   to all but our very own

Moonmilk

icon

tide pool
gas stove
the sea
pentazocine sea
studying seas
desirous

then met the poet
and her mouth lifts air

the higher

sun twists/
            fires
hot light/
            claws
black and bone
            of clouds/
sings through
            ribs of rain
to the ground/
            seed/
beneath
            blooming

a succulent/   somewhere
to the left of the buried tongue:
a poem/   another motherless Eve

songs of prey

she comes
wearing a poet's fire coat
talon & tango
fang & fandango
in her eyes
pearls dive and whirl
I open
she nips my tongue
words ignite
her harrier wings
bleed & burn

conceptual installations
for sandi

stab of brush   cut of paint
rusty hasp   a burnt match
arms of whitened wood   your blood on the cross

my lungs empty breathing your name
I watch your work
stretching across rage and jubilation
convulse across lands and language
to the body to skin
and its openings
to the culpable uterus
splitting secrets
staining lies
and saving
saving the babies

children come

                    dontcha wanna tip the moonglass
               drink it dry
          so do I
     so do I

               moonmilk for the hungry

for sarah

rich
in descent
of night
a child
in the wide
field
spreads fire
arms stick/
white
roots of
moonwillow
revealed

elegia

fatcat dandies by
belly sways
swallow's tail
tufts her widebrim jaw
light falls into her
daedalian eyes
green visions swell
across the field
carcass fires float
a ghostly lake
on morning air

blue canoe

tracers of light
   chink the waves
the lake sways
   a fabulist
rhinestone fire
   its thick edges
furling and swelling
   lily, cattail
skirt and frill

I am a gemcutter
   culling jewels
a renegade shim
   of a loose bluemoon
my blue canoe
   slurs the surface
hewing light
   from deep night
waterhard sky

lune

faint lisping jazz notes swirl the air   late night
half moon   & the moon coda rings clarion clear
still night   lunar rule
words do no good at all

moon waxing   coming time   & the white hanging thirst
in the black night   will be sated

will be full and rolling about   a fat bubble gurgling
message sent   message received

here   we are grounded in terror   checking the phones
trying the lights   turning the radio ON

moon waning
shanks of her boomerang round the sun   she jabbers on
complaining   coming back back to herself

she skitters across the sea
wailing at our walls of disaffection

she does not know   we've composed a cavatina in black
along her wicked tail

siege

aphids graze my stumpy plants
caterpillars smorg the trees
ants saw the studded walls

poetry is my diversion   using
bent spoons   files   anything
I write above the din

shut your hole honey, mine's making money

I i want man love i want that male
thing in the language genetic syn
tax decorative lines
of forests and arrows
and brooks runnelling into the bosom of the sea
i want that response in reading women
ahs and oohs
yes and
give me a woman with a ferrari heart who
buys the metaphor goddesses be damned
re/claim/ation be damned
i want that nether power, that
clout waking the loins,
tooling the engine of my beloved

II   iter iter
i want to ride all the roman roads un/quest/tioned
and conquer with my hidden
tongue my
man tongue deceptive, soft
with words of silk with
words of love
i want this classical novel for my life
textual serpents be damned poeming be damned father tongue
slip
into me
tongue i can count on quixote
quixote; centuries in the picaresque; millennia in the morals;
i want aquinas
augustine and sartre (pepper my
victuals with voltaire) i'll be
a pet of meta physics, i want him
singing in my entrails reading me
like a chicken (prophetically foul)
russell and saint paul
merton and kafka officianados right
hand man

III women will shake
me down for shakespeare   i'll
sing their tune and She
will come and   buy
this emerging voice
i'll be her hero
be her man   i'll get
what i want what's my due
and write it   She'll
wear stiletto heels for me
menstruate in another room   while i
work out my man love on
paper   apply
that thing in the language
stickhandle into her
recalcitrant heart   pop
her net   tickle her twine   and
score by jesus score;
i'll be the man who
writes of women
and wins the booker
prize

instruments of wood and wind

a high wind hits the stand of pine and a kind of spectacular
applause ensues. you stand off to the left in a clearing at the
edge of the cliff;

ah, the wind, you say,

blasts of it stiff against you. your blondshocked hair whips
your jaw and mouth. your sweater tightens, your body jerks
in the marionette dance of gusts and lulls.

this high place belongs to you. this sea below, a bowl of
darting light, catches all the blue from your glitter eyes.
moss, pillow green, swarms at your feet. this world is yours.
you have travelled always here, stood here, an outcrop of
beauty and will.

I have seen eagles sway back on the wind at the shout of
your laughter,

I have seen the tide draw away like a grinning mouth when
you lifted your arms,

I have seen you drink from a milky cloud that scudded the
clean sky at your bidding, and foamed your cheeks with its
spume of water and air.

and I have seen the trees shrug out of the shadows and stand
with you naked, their bark a sudden sheen, their limbs
spinning a parasol over your head.

———————

the high wind falls. your body is loose and trembling. the
tremors rise like wavelets, like surf, until you shimmer in
the quick stillness. another wind starts somewhere, it runs
under the sky at you. I hear it. it has the roar of distant
highway violence in its throat.

you, I know, are waiting.

this javelin wind arcs and hums; a single speeding note. it
hits you. the trees around you are stripped of bark and their
dark blood is slow to surface in such giant wounds. but you

grow thin and flat and hard.

you grow deceptive as paper birch and for a moment I think
you will outlast the fists and kicks of your beloved wind.

you open the flat of your mouth; your tongue rips through
the sheet of your face,

you fly apart –

you fly apart –

the wind rolls and throws itself down the receding chins of
rock and thunders into the calm sea.

I've fallen and lie clenched as a sea star to this green moss.
there is nothing in the air; no movement or sound or smell. I
open an eye; the lashes sweep the spines of a nestling pine
cone.

Middle Distance

inversion

when did those eyes slant
& skew like gulag's gate

how did the heart revivify   detonate
what is this deuce grin
teeth beating time

                    I hang on the hook
                    I spread my legs

I trash cells and cells
of memory

your face barks/
language blows
up heaving
blacks the two shouldered sky

where is the red fibre
where is that tonsil of light/
how in this tunnel can air be swallowed
how in this renascent womb could a mind

                  clap
                  &
                  close

in that old deadhorse dream
danseuses lift and grind:
The Dance Without Torso
The Jive
cut down at the knees

fire chinks and tinkles
combustible mirth
there in that sucking tunnel of birth
we fly/
my symbio
we die

balletto

under
the blade
of a crystal thigh
blood limns
the edges of
delicate wounds
drops one red
medallion to the floor
then two
three
four/   the fifth
is black
as ink
a pinwheel/   a child's
sun
kiss
scalpel tongue/   be done

middle distance

I am between walls
right now
cats and longdead dogs
(I go through dogs like a chainsaw)

I am between covenants
a kind of x betwixt the vows

I am between kitchen and front door
when your beautiful hand
descends
throws panda posters
into the oven
docks the time   time is up
loses the shopping list, loses the children
launders the cheque
and guts
the bottom drawer

e/jacu/lation

sexual energy
electric river
confluent passion
inexorable orgasm

I mean:
I break the boneless back of your dying

cantabile

you fuck my ear with your tongue
sub   lingua   canticle of sweet patois

melodies bloom in this chamber
of the deaf   vibrato on a pelvic drum

your breath wets my neck   orgasm falls
plaited by my fingerbraids

we answer the upheaval   the unseen
my hands sleep still   canaries in a cave

scissure

I sun lattices your face
   in white and shadow
   your eyes switch
   cat tails
   you are
   a figurine
   a knick knack lost
   deep in your bric a brac chair

II I close my eye
   my heart spins
   a tempest
   like solar wind
   a hail of blood cells
   until cells shoot
   into stars
   white against black extremity

III soot shoals one wingboned cheek
   I stoop
   unravel a web
   that whiskers your hand
   your eyes arch and sigh
   loosed from some jittery watch
   this un weaving this
   splint er ing a
   float
   in the
   room

iv heartspin
    firestorm
    sears the back
    of the eye to blue
    the face   the garroted throat
    the children
    hack at the noose
    mommy takes them
    bears them up
    split suns across
    atomic sky

v   the earth bulges towards the moon
    I am drowning
    you are high and dry

discarnate

the mouth
the lips
your kiss
the jaw
unhinged
the tongue
around
my neck

the teeth
eat
the sound

my face
splits in
two
I look
both ways

twentysome

she is so young   she is pastel
pink meadows are her landscape   fruity seas
dawn romps from her throat   she laughs like a bell
her orgasms always come back
pistol sprints   in slo mo intensity

under the sun of my need
her palliatives cook up like gold
hooves beat the air over my head
when she arcs and suckles old kisses
from my breasts

she holds everything in her eyes
her fine arms spin me to sleep
our limbs twine   bloom
wisteria   in the morning
envined   I am unlaced by
her tongue and roguish fingers

overnight   she is Gaia strafing the moon

turn me loose

oh give me the honeybunch baby blues
trash my foos/ball
me babe   back me right up
and sing me the news

ring of fire

all those years we stood at the crater's rim hurling desire
down the throat of our dormant love. staring.

so much craving. the belly of the mountain began to churn
and boil and explode.

you erupted in a spume of liquid flame. you flew up, entire,
transformed, and began to dance along the tongues of fire.
you reeled away.

from where I stood, through the ash, sun blackened (clinging
as I was to the edge, to the lip) I could not see your
fingersnap, your hiphop abandon, your leap.

I was too frantic, finding my lava feet.

concertina

you got the picture?
your heart threw you from bed
slammed feet to the floor
dead/
run

got the picture?
you thought it a dream
all that bop/ discordant jazz
caco/
phone

the picture?
your mouth sang real sang red
the brain's clean now, pain's
clean now

picture?
the flamingo fling in my life
the curt beautiful riff in my
eclectic
guitar

wanna go dancin before you fly?

natasha

and you kneel
plunging stars
into my heart so
I cannot bear
the swelling of the night
except to spin
light from my bones
and guide your aim

TRISH BIRNEY

Cherie Geauvreau was born in Windsor in 1948. She has excellent writer's credentials, having been a cook, a house cleaner and a forklift operator, and having worked in pharmaceuticals and restaurant management. She also served short stints in various institutions of higher learning and in the convent. She lives on the West Coast where she writes in a small cabin in the woods and works in her community as a fierce advocate for women and children. Her work was featured in the 20th Anniversary *Capilano Review*, as well as *Prism International, The American Voice* and *Prairie Fire*, among others. This is her first book.